Learning to Read in
English and Spanish
Made Easy

──── WORKBOOK ────

A Guide for Teachers, Tutors, and Parents

By: Susie G. Navarijo

Learning to Read in English and Spanish Made Easy
Copyright © 2022 by Susie G. Navarijo

All rights reserved. No part of this book may be reproduced or transmitted in any form or by any means, electronic or mechanical, including photocopying, recording, or by any information storage and retrieval system without express written permission from the author, except in the case of brief quotations embodied in critical reviews and certain other noncommercial uses permitted by copyright law.

Printed in the United States of America.

Brilliant Books Literary
137 Forest Park Lane Thomasville
North Carolina 27360 USA

This book is dedicated to my children, my grandchildren, and the many ex-students who inspired me to write it. It is also dedicated to my husband, who was so supportive.

Table of Contents

Introduction vii
Reading in a Bilingual Classroom 1
Getting to the Root of the Problem 3
Getting Through 5
First Things First 6
The Home Connection 8
Comprehension and Fluency 9
The Three Modalities of Learning 11
Phonics 15
Letter Sound Associations 17
A Different Approach to Reading 25
Writing the Letters 30
Vowel Lessons Using Charts 38
Endings to Root Words 64
Conjugating Verbs 66
Making Complete Sentences 67
Spanish Reading 68

Introduction

There is no one way to teach reading to every child. So much depends on the child's learning style, on the child's experiences, and on the teacher's teaching style. In my thirty-five years of teaching first grade and tutoring individuals and small groups in my class, I have learned to have a variety of tricks at hand in order to reinforce and re-teach some lessons. Sometimes, all one has to do is look into the eyes of some children to know that teacher and child are not connecting. The necessity of transmitting information from the teacher's brain to the child's brain requires a repertoire of ideas at hand in order to meet the needs of each individual. In this way, every child has a better chance of experiencing success. After all, that is the most important aspect of teaching: to reach each child's individual potential, thus leaving no one behind.

If a child in my class was having problems, I would sometimes invite the parent to school for the day or visit them at home, not to complain about the child, but to show them that their family was important to me. Bringing out the positive aspects of a child, as well as his weaknesses, is important. Parent and child respond positively and accept what the teacher has to say. I have made many good friends from the parents of my children. Many have been room mothers who were able to help their own children as well as others by using the strategies they observed in the classroom.

Every principal for whom I worked has recognized that I had very high expectations for every child. They were right. I did expect every child to learn. I made many mistakes as a teacher, but believing in my children was not one of them. It was always my goal to take them from where they were and guide them towards their potential. I learned that not everyone's potential is the same. But sometimes, we shortchange children by not expecting them to do more.

Teachers have often told me I should write a book about the ideas I have developed throughout the years. New teachers come to school with little or no experience. They may find it necessary to tutor some of the children in their classroom. So this is my way of sharing my experience with new teachers as well as other tutors, parent helpers, and individuals.

These ideas will be useful to mothers helping their children at home. Many mothers have come to me to ask me how they can help their child. I always tell them that first of all, reading to them is the most important thing they can do. Reading, talking, and playing helps children to become better listeners. It also helps them to practice language patterns, grammar, and vocabulary. Experiencing their world through play enables children to concretely see what they will later learn abstractly. Pictures in the mind are formed from experiencing the world first hand. This gives children the foundation for reading.

Reading in a Bilingual Classroom

My ideas for teaching English reading are unique and effective. Spanish reading is less complex than English so I will give an overview of reading in Spanish after I introduce some points in writing, spelling, and grammar in English. But throughout the book, I will relate English to Spanish reading and some problems one might encounter along the way. As a bilingual teacher, I found it necessary to teach reading in English to some children who also knew how to speak Spanish and reading in Spanish to a group of children who knew little or no English. This was in addition to teaching English to monolingual students. Dividing my time was challenging at best, but my students seemed to progress rather smoothly in both languages.

Teaching two languages allowed me to compare the strategies used in both languages and to alter the methods suggested in most reading texts to better serve my students. This led me to seek commonalities and to reinforce learning by repeating the same concepts in English and in Spanish whenever possible. For example, instead of teaching the short vowel sound, I found it effective to teach all the sounds for each vowel simultaneously. The Spanish children were making syllables—ma me mi mo mu—to make words, so I had a chart for them. The English children were making syllables (or small words) with a ai au - m**a**n m**ai**l m**au**l, so I had a chart for them. When it was time to transition from Spanish to English, I could then point out that the three sounds of "a" had the short vowel sound as in apple, the long vowel sound as in its name, and that the third sound was much like the "ah" in Spanish. By memorizing the three sounds and referring to the chart for the particular spelling of "a," in an unknown word children could figure out a word they did not know, instead of asking the teacher all the time. It made them more independent readers.

Many of the ideas presented in this book are a conglomeration of lessons that have been developed from scratch or have been derived from bits and pieces of different lessons from my thirty years experience as a first grade teacher. Some methods generally used in Spanish, I used in English. It was simpler that way. I wanted to be consistent so that the children would learn from each other—many of the sounds after all, are the same. I wanted to use the strengths I found in one program to help me with the other language. This way, there was less confusion during the transition from Spanish reading to English reading.

The charts and explanations are simple and memorable. They can easily be used for students at any level or any age. I have encountered third and fourth graders who benefited from many of the ideas and charts in this book. I even used them with a ninth grader who was learning English as a second language. Tutors who need to help students catch up in their reading will find these charts useful. New teachers will be able to fill in the gaps found in many teacher editions. Room mothers can learn ways to help in the classroom as well as at home. Students of all ages coming from another country, or those who just want to strengthen their phonics skills, will benefit from these ideas.

Bilingual children do not have to be scared of reading in their second language. Not every child is ready to transition into English at the same time. For some, it takes longer. But once they have a good grasp of their first language, they will find themselves listening in to the lessons of the other language. This is when a teacher will turn them on by allowing them to join in. I feel bilingual students ready to read in English will find this way of learning to read much easier. The repetition used in the charts is helpful because it reinforces the English sounds with rhyming words.

Some of the examples of children I have had in my room may be extreme cases, and pre-kinder and kindergarten classes have eliminated many problems a first grade teacher used to encounter many years ago. But every new teacher should see the importance of experience. I realize some of the ideas presented in this book may already be used by teachers elsewhere. Every good teacher will grab ideas from many places, change some of them, and discard others. I have done this, but I have mostly made up little stories and charts that have developed into what I have presented in this book. I hope you enjoy them and find them useful.

Getting to the Root of the Problem

When I began teaching first grade, I taught a child who could not learn the alphabet. It was November, and all the many hints, clues, associations, and individual tutoring I gave her did not help. I explained in English and in Spanish. She could not remember the sound of a single letter. There had to be something missing. Something was wrong—not with the child—but with my way of teaching this individual. She had attended kinder, but at that time kindergarten students were not retained. I decided to go to kinder and learn their curriculum in order to find the missing link. I was determined to find out how to best help her.

One of the first things I evaluated her on was categorizing. To my surprise, I immediately realized she could not categorize at all. She could not put colors into any sort of grouping when compared with other objects. She could not group the different colors themselves. These are pre-reading skills and should be mastered before attempting formal reading.

In my class, I had a wall space with letters and their sounds and a different area with numbers and pictures representing quantities. I had a bulletin board with shapes and a bulletin board with colors.

If this child did not separate in her mind the symbols associated with reading from the ones that had to do with numbers and shapes, then, how could she grab from all these possibilities the ones needed for reading? They were all jumbled in her brain, and she did not know from where to grab. Deeper still, if she could not categorize simple things like letters, numbers, colors, and shapes, then how could she differentiate from the meaning of reading itself in order to know what the teacher expected from her?

I immediately began numerous lessons before school and after school. I discussed the vocabulary and concepts needed such as number, shape, letter, etc. She needed to know what a shape was before she could even understand to what group it belonged. Not right away, but with diligence and persistence, there was a breakthrough. A short time after she learned to categorize, she learned the letters and their sounds. I reminded her, before every lesson, that these symbols were the only ones on which she had to concentrate because these particular symbols were needed for reading. She started to feel success. For the first time, she understood what was expected from her.

In the end, she realized people can communicate in many ways. They can communicate with voice, with gestures, and with symbols like pictures or writing. Reading is like talking to someone, but with symbols. All one needs to do in order to read symbols is to learn the code. This child had now begun to break the code. This child was not going to be left behind.

Getting Through

Breaking the code for this child in as short a time as possible required a lot of creativity. She needed to catch up with the other children and the regular lessons from the school were sometimes not enough for her. I wanted to invent something that would be meaningful. Just like one associates the "M" of McDonalds with hamburgers, a child can associate a letter with something with which he or she is familiar. Many texts have since come out with ways to associate some of the sounds. This is good! Different children remember some associations better than others. So, if one association did not work, I would try to think of another.

I began to associate the sounds with something familiar to her. I would scribble things down on a paper until I found something that clicked. Tricks like these helped her to associate sounds to something in her world because she had nothing else on which to base them. This point is important to remember.

These associations proved to be very helpful for my student. But not until she realized which symbols to use for reading and which to use during math did she realize that numbers were representing quantities and they were used to count and put quantities together. The letters were used for reading. What a lesson for a new teacher! Every new teacher should realize that it is up to us to be creative and find ways of reaching children.

The Letter Sound Associations beginning on page twenty-four are the result of trying to get through to this child. Some have been refined through the years, but generally they remained the same because they worked.

First Things First

College courses had taught me that learning is sequential. But there is nothing like experience to really bring home the point. One needs to teach at the child's level, making sure any essential gaps are filled. This, also, is a very important point. Filling in gaps is like fixing a wall of bricks with the bottom layer missing a few vital bricks. The next layers are not going to have a solid base. The higher one goes, the more the problems will begin to show. This is why many children begin to have problems in reading. But if the gaps are filled, the child will have a strong foundation on which to build.

Gaps are not always easy to recognize. Sometimes, it might be a lack of vocabulary development or concept development. I have encountered children who did not know words such as "alike" and "different." Concepts associated with alike and different are essential in recognizing letters. This is another pre-reading skill a child needs to learn before going into formal reading.

The b and the d are **alike** because they both have a line and a circle. But they are **different** because of the **position** of the circle in relation to the line. Sometimes children do not see this, so it is our job as teachers and tutors to point it out to them.

The capital J and the lower case j are alike in that they both look like a hook. The **position** of the j is **different** because one stands on the baseline and the other sits on the baseline and has its tail hanging down.

The capital S and the lower case s are **alike** in shape, but the size is different, and size is what makes one a capital S, the one used at the beginning of sentences and at the beginning of special names.

If a child keeps making mistakes, check to see if they understand the concept of same and different or of some other vocabulary word.

Kinder and first grades teach differences in size, shape, and position. Recognizing differences in size, shape, and position help children to learn letters. Unless a child understands the concept associated with this vocabulary, then the d and the b are both b, or they are both d.

Fortunately, most children either come to school knowing the concept of these words (alike and different), or they quickly learn it in pre-kinder or kindergarten. But if every child learned every lesson they were supposed to, there would not be a need for tutors.

There are many reasons why a student may fall behind and need a tutor. Circumstances are such that, through no fault of his own, a child may be absent for a prolonged time or go through a crisis which makes him temporarily inattentive. He may be sleepy while an important lesson is being taught. Extreme shyness also may interfere with learning, as will extreme sensitivity to criticism. Whatever the reason, we as teachers and as tutors are now responsible for filling those gaps which are causing them to fall behind. Besides, many children who need tutoring need tutoring for a short time. Once some gaps are filled, some children can just take off.

A teacher may teach in an area where she/he will never encounter a child who has a need for tutors, but rest assured that many schools do need tutors. And with the way the population moves around now, there is no doubt children with special needs are found in every area. With the growing Latino populations, schools need a quick way to get children caught up with English reading once they are ready. I repeat: once they are ready. I have taught children who caught on to their second language after four to six months. That was a very special family. It takes much longer for the rest of us. But once children have a firm grip on what reading entails in their own language, the transition is much smoother. After all, trying to concentrate on meaning while the mind is preoccupied with new sounds, new vocabulary, and new rules is a very tough task for people of any age, not to mention young children. It might be surprising to see how many children are accused of not listening or not able to learn because of lack of understanding by the teacher. So, after categorizing is taken care of, the language barriers are broken, and all the gaps are filled, the child is more ready to learn to read.

May I mention again how beneficial it is to be in contact with the child's parent? I remember my sixth grade English teacher coming to my house to let my mom know how I was doing. She sat down and talked to my mom as if she were a friend. It made a big impression on me.

The Home Connection

Vocabulary enrichment and reading go hand in hand, and it is essential that the child have a sense of story. This is the very first step in learning to read and most times begins at home. A story sense is developed when a child understands that something is going to happen to someone or to something in the story. That character has a personality. The story has a setting. And the ending of the story is anticipated because the child wants to know how the problem is going to be resolved.

Reading to the class is important for all children but especially for children with needs. Many children who come to school with a high vocabulary have heard a variety of words because someone read to them. They need to hear stories at home, but some do not. They need to have vocabulary enrichment, but many children are not spoken to in complete sentences at home. This is why there can never be enough reading and storytelling in the kinder and first grades.

Programs like AVANCE, developed by Dr. Gloria Rodriguez, in San Antonio, Texas, have been created to help parents prepare their children for school. It focuses on the parent as the child's first and most important teacher. In her book, *Raising Nuestros Ninos,* Dr. Rodriguez expounds on pre-readiness activities needed in order to get ready for the formal instruction at school.

For example, children need to be allowed to explore and experiment in order to develop certain concepts. AVANCE stresses the importance of learning these concepts through play. Concrete experiences pave the way to understanding the verbal concept. This type of transition leads to emotional stability. When a child tackles a project like reading without the necessary background, emotional stability is hindered and the child will feel insecure in his ability to learn.

Comprehension and Fluency

I once had a child who could decode words, but had absolutely no idea of what he had read. He could sound out words fluently enough for a first grader, but he could not tell me what the story, the paragraph, or the sentence was about. This too was an extreme case, yes, but brings home another point. After reading the same short story many times, he could still not tell me the "who," the "what," or the "where" of one simple sentence, much less of a three or four sentence paragraph. There was something missing, and I was going to find it.

I decided to try something else—drawing. The story had pictures, but they meant nothing to him. We took one sentence: a simple sentence. The story was talking about a boy going home. I took the boy's name in the story, switched it with his own name, and used it in the exact sentence. I took him to a mirror and showed him the "star" of this story.

I asked him to draw a picture of himself on a full-size paper while looking into the mirror. The "star" of the story was going to "do" something. The verb in the sentence brought on a lesson on how he moved. This was what the "star" did. I had him act it out in the room. Then I had him draw arrows in the picture to show movement. His feet were bent to also show movement. We changed the verb and had him moving in different ways. In one sentence, he walked. In another sentence, he skipped, then flew and crawled. He was going home, so he drew the picture of his house. We drew his family inside the house. Now the sentence was his story.

Every sentence thereafter was "connected" to the first sentence in some way. Each time a new sentence was read, we discussed in particular how that sentence was connected to the first and second sentences, etc. I made little arrows to show how pronouns referred to some word that had already been used in the sentences before. This was so much fun for the whole class. We practiced this as much as possible. Soon, his little finger would move back and forth, while he made "connections" from one part of the story to the other.

All this painstaking, step by step, procedure was fruitful because he was a kinesthetic learner. He acted out one sentence at a time, and it became real to him. He now had a connection to the sentence. It was not necessary to do this for too much longer—only when he had trouble with a particular sentence. But we now had a springboard for comprehension. He could put himself in the story because children are basically egocentric. This means they see themselves as the center of the universe and the world revolves around them. In making this young boy the center of the story, he experienced the story from within, making it easier to go outside his world in order to experience the story. He made a connection to the outside world through movement, because the action involved made him move. This made sense to him. He could now develop a "sense of story."

The Three Modalities of Learning

Kinesthetic Learners

This method was good for him. It involved movement and he liked it. Kinesthetic learners learn best through movement. They remember things better when they are in the middle of the action. Role playing is an excellent learning tool for kinesthetic learners. Acting out problems in math, cutting, drawing, as well as making things that have to do with stories, etc, help a child to remember things better.

Auditory Learners

Auditory learners can learn best by hearing things. I have had children who did not seem to be listening because their eyes were wandering elsewhere. But when I asked them to repeat what I had just taught, they did it without a blink of the eye. Some auditory learners are very lucky to be able to do this. Auditory learners will remember details that they have heard (phone numbers, oral directions, speeches, lectures, etc.) much better than other children.

Visual Learners

Visual learners learn better through sight. If they see it in picture or in writing, they retain things better. As a second grader, I was extremely shy and did not know enough English to get by. I had learned to tune out much of my world. Perhaps I did this because I did not understand all of what was said, or because of my extreme shyness, or maybe because of both these reasons. At this early age, I rarely made eye contact with others.

But one day in the second grade, I caught sight of the teacher writing math problems on the board. It had to do with regrouping in addition and subtraction. I did not understand all of what she was saying, but I watched every step. The next day, I was one of only a few who understood how to add two digit numbers. The teacher had me teach the other children. Being a tutor for the first time was a wonderful experience for me. Not only did it make me an even stronger mathematician, it helped me to open up to other children.

I was obviously a better visual learner than an auditory learner at this particular time in my life. One can practice to get better at the other modalities later, but if one recognizes their strengths as a young child, those strengths will help in the meantime, until the other modalities are strengthened.

Many children are able to use, and benefit from, all three methods of learning. They are good listeners and are able to focus on what they hear. They are not distracted easily with noise around them. They are able to focus on what they see and learn from it. And working things out with their hands, etc., helps them to internalize what they have learned. They are very lucky.

But some children seem to learn mainly through one or two learning modalities (auditory, visual, or kinesthetic). That does not mean that they will always need special instruction in their particular strength, but for now, at this particular time in their lives, it is important to use it whenever possible. This is part of meeting a child's need. Every modality should be practiced because children learn through all their senses: sight, hearing, taste, smell, and touch. Each modality will become stronger with practice.

Reviewing the Pictures

Before beginning to read a story, a very good strategy to use is to review the pictures with the child. Preview the pictures and discuss what they think is happening. Before turning the page, ask them what they think is going to happen next. This is called "predicting what comes next." Also, elicit some of the vocabulary words used in the story. Children with low vocabulary skills cannot come up with vocabulary they have never heard. When they come across these words in the story, they will figure them out better because you have already discussed those words.

Context Clues

While reading a story, children should try to figure out an unknown word by the content of the sentence. The words surrounding an unknown word, as well as the beginning sound of a word, give clues to figure out the unknown word. It has to make sense in the sentence. If they do not have to stop and sound out words letter by letter, the child can better concentrate on the meaning. But if they do have to stop and figure out a word, it is a good idea to get them to repeat the sentence from the beginning. Fluency will be improved and the meaning will not be lost. Remember that many children have to do many things simultaneously. Not only are they decoding sounds, but they have to deal with vocabulary and sentence structures with which they may not be familiar.

Using these methods to better comprehend will also help in reading fluency. Fluency helps comprehension because it is the natural way of talking. When one can anticipate which words are to be used, they will be able to make good guesses when they come across a word they do not know.

Remember, children who are read to often become better listeners. Good listeners are more focused on what is being said and its meaning.

Responding to Questions

While checking on comprehension, either in a story or in a test, make sure that the student knows what is expected in the answer. Ask him who, what, when, where, why questions—but make sure that they know that a "who" question is asking for a person and that a "why" question is asking for a reason, etc. There are many times when we may ask: "In this story, who was running?" and get an answer that goes something like, "He went to the house." Obviously, the child was not focused on the "who" part of the question, because he responded with a "where" answer. That is one of the main reasons for errors in testing.

The Brain

Whenever inattentiveness disrupted learning in my classroom, I reminded my children of how they learned. Learning takes place when something from the outside comes into the brain through the five senses. In order for it to stay, it must connect to something else that is already in the brain. It was important to look at me, because they would learn through their eyes. If I was pointing to something on the board, for example, they could not make the "connection" in their brain because their eyes were not sending that message to their brain. So even though they may hear what is being said, the brain does not know what to connect it to. It was a lost opportunity to connect what was said with what was seen. If they moved around or talked while I was instructing, they could not make a connection because their ears were not sending the message to their brain to connect with something that was already in the brain. What I had to say was very important, so they had to try to deliberately make that connection in the brain.

This is the way I explained learning, as connections in the brain. There are certain parts in the brain that accept what comes in from the eyes, and a different part of the brain accepts what comes in from the ears, etc. When visual images come into the brain through the eyes, they land and form a dot in the brain. They try to hold on, but if there is nothing to connect to, that "dot" will soon disappear.

Sometimes, there are past experiences that the child has had that will allow for this connection to take place—sometimes there are not. But if one **says** a sound at the same time that they are **looking** at it, the *auditory dot* will make a connection with the *visual dot*. The link between visual and auditory dots is what makes information stick. Learning takes place because the dots make a link and do not disappear. Then by writing the letter while saying the sound, the *touch dot* will connect to the visual and auditory dots.

So, children are encouraged to write while saying the sound of the letter in order to make a strong connection in the brain.

People with many connections know many things, so their brain is all wrinkly like a raisin. Babies, when they are born, have a smooth brain because they do not have many connections yet. They have not learned to walk, talk, hold their spoon, etc.

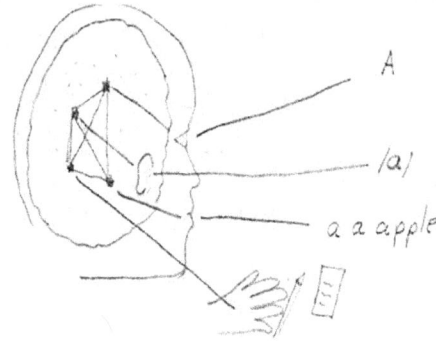

I make lines coming from their surroundings to the tongue, the eyes, the ears, the hand, and nose. When they see an "A" for example, it goes through their eyes to the area in the brain that accepts visual stimuli. There, the image of the "A" is represented by a dot. The dot represents learning only if it connects to another dot in the brain.

The brain is full of connections. Many times throughout my career children have suddenly sat up and announced that they had made a connection while pointing to their brain. Others would quiet their noisy friends and tell them that they had to be quiet and concentrate in order to make connections. These are truly some of the rewards of teaching.

Phonics

I believe strongly in phonics. One cannot make meaningful sentences through phonics alone. But I do believe that some children need it in order to keep up with their peers. Everyone benefits from it. I knew a teacher who did not believe in phonics. She felt that children could absorb reading "naturally" through listening to stories, the way her daughter had learned. It was December, and only a few children in her class had learned to read or write. She was obviously wrong. Not everyone learns naturally, not everyone learns through sight words, and not everyone learns to read through phonics alone. It takes a little bit of everything. But for some children, phonics is the key that unlocks the door to successful reading.

Teaching all the letters to the whole class is sometimes unnecessary. Some children come to school knowing all letters and some come to school knowing some letters. By evaluating, those that know can be challenged with independent work, while the teacher works with those that need more help.

Of course, not just the sounds, but the names of the letters are also important. The alphabet should be recited daily. Many times the alphabet is memorized in a robotic manner, so that no one letter is associated with its name. The L, M, N, O, P becomes M, M, M, O, P, for example. To overcome this, I had the children point to and say the alphabet backwards. If they could do this, I knew which letters they really knew and could concentrate on those letters that they did not know. I could also give more time to the other children who needed more help.

The vowels should also be recited daily as a group. The y is sometimes used as a vowel. There are many children I have tutored who did not know the vowels. It is easy to see why they needed tutoring. Somewhere down the line, their reading progress broke down because they lacked a crucial part of putting sounds together to make words.

Most curriculums introduce small stories that encompass a limited vocabulary with a limited number of consonants that are introduced first along with one, or maybe two, short vowel sounds. Of course, a few sight words are always needed in order to make complete sentences. Sight words like "the," "is," "to," and "a" are introduced gradually. The "short a" words will contain the consonants M, S, T, and/or P. Children learn a few simple words using these letters. They then gradually add more consonants along with the "short e" sound. All the short vowel sounds are introduced in this manner. With a few more consonants each time, a new short vowel sound is presented, and more words are introduced.

After all the short vowel sounds are learned, the long vowel sounds are introduced with the use of the "silent e" at the end of a word. Then, a separate lesson introduces the "ee" and/or the "ea," and another lesson introduces the "ow" and/or the "ou," etc.

In teaching Spanish reading, however, the vowels are introduced first. The consonants M, S, T, and P are introduced and used as syllables with the vowels. The syllables are then combined to make words. Consonants are added gradually. With more syllables, more combinations are possible to make more words. I really like this method of making words. So let's begin with the vowels in English

Letter Sound Associations

The Vowels

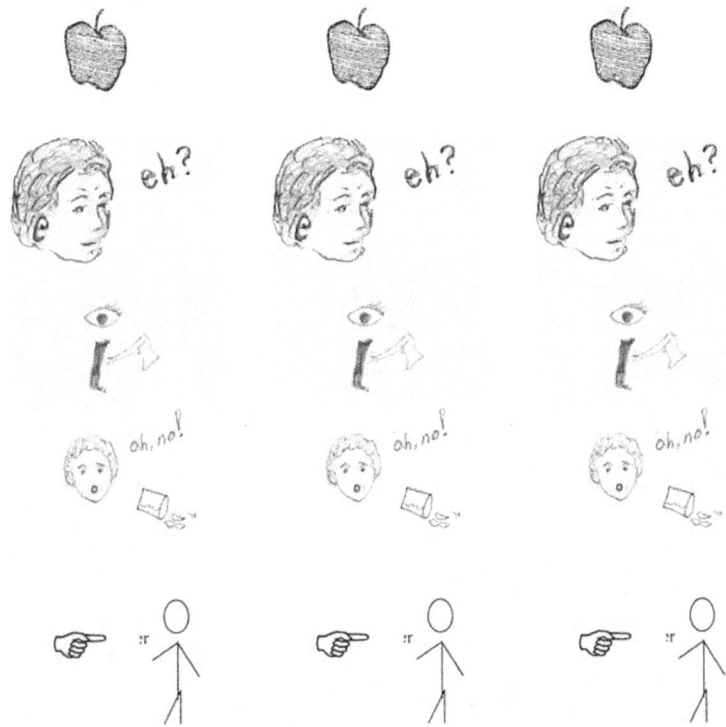

The a is an aa-apple that says /"ah"/ cause it's good.

The e is an ear on the face of an old lady who cannot hear. She keeps asking, "Eh?" If you notice, an actual ear does look like a small e.

The i has an eye drawn around the dot. Its short vowel sound is choppy, as if it were cut in half with an ax.

The o is a round mouth opened by a child who spilled orange juice and said "Oh, no!" The round mouth goes big and small to make the two sounds of o.

The U is a finger pointing to you (u).

Punch yourself in the stomach while You say "uh" for the short sound of u and "ooh" 'cause it hurt.

Other Vowel Families

The er, ir, and er are the **/er/ girl triplets**. They have cousins "ear" as in earn and "wor" in word.

The cOW said "OUch"

The Consonants

There is a cute story that goes with the b, d, and p.
These stories have always helped children remember the b, d, and p.

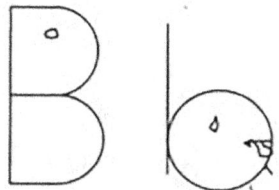

The capital B and the small b are facing in the same direction because while trying to talk to each other, they both make soft popping sounds and the small b turns in order not to be bobbed in the face.

The capital D and the small d are looking at each other because they do not have that problem. They talk dddddd all day long without worries. At this time I pretend to be a capital D and start speaking ddd talk with the child and encourage her to talk dddd back to me.

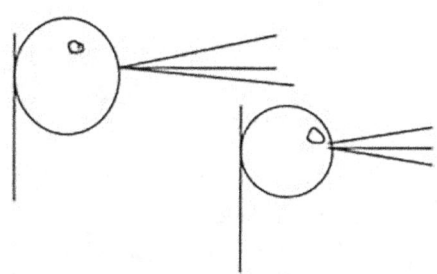

The capital P, on the other hand, does a big popping sound and scares the small p, so he ducks down and turns in order not to be popped in the face.

Wrap the c around the eye. Say, " I can see you with a c" Put the c around your throat. Mimic choking using the hard sound of the c.

Point to the horizontal line on the f while showing the way the lips meet the teeth in a horizontal position to make the fff sound.

The g is a little girl with long hair going down her side. Stress the /g/ sound.

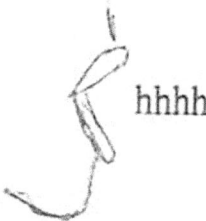 hhhh

The h is air coming out of your throat.

The j is half of a jump rope. It is called the jumping J.

Learning to Read in English and Spanish Made Easy

The kicking K has a kicking leg that just kicked the kickball.

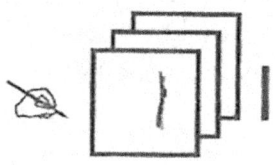

The l is a lllong lllline going down the page. Stress the lll sound as you push your finger down the page.

The n is the nail of a finger.

The q is a cute queen looking back. The word "cute" is a hint to its name.

The V is the victory sign made with your fingers.

U + U = W (double the u)

The w is double the u, (The u is written like this in many places).

x_____

The x "marks the spot". It marks the spot where we make mistakes. It also marks the spot for a signature, etc.

The y is a yoyo with a string coming down.

z z z zoom

The z is the zoom of a jet. The Z is the voiced sound of s.

Consonant Digraphs

The consonant digraphs (sh, ch, th, wh) need to be given special attention when working with Spanish speaking children since the th, the sh, and the wh do not exist in Spanish reading. The ch **is** in the Spanish alphabet, so there is no problem with its sound.

Sh The sh sound was compared with the ch sound using a balloon. If you blow up a balloon and let the air out slowly, the sound will come out smoothly because there is nothing blocking the way. The same thing with your mouth. If you keep your tongue down, the air sound comes out smoothly.

Ch If while making the sh sound with the balloon, you quickly pinch the opening and let go, a sound comes out that can be compared with the ch sound. Point out that the tongue taps up sharply to close the air flow—just like in the balloon—making the ch sound.

Th While making the th sound, you bite your tongue softly and blow. If you "voice" the sound, it tickles your tongue as in the word the. If you do not "voice" the sound as in the "think," it does not tickle your tongue. A voiced sound is one where a vibration is felt in the throat while the sound is being made.

Wh The wh sound is the "turn around" sound. Sometimes, you hear the h sound before the w sound as in "where." You only hear the w sound in "wharf."

Other Consonant Rules

As I have said before, the consonant y can also be used as a vowel. It is usually at the end of a word when it is used as a vowel to make the sound of a long e (when at the end of a two or more syllable word), or a long i (when at the end of a one syllable word). However, there are some words, like bicycle, where the y is in the middle of a word, but is used as a vowel.

There are two consonants that have more than one consonant sound— the letter c and the letter g. Each of these letters can have a hard sound or a soft sound. The soft g and soft c will have the vowel e or the vowel i after them. The hard g and hard c will have the vowel a, or the vowel o, or the vowel u after them.

The problem comes with the letter g. There are several important words that do not follow the rule. After practicing words that do follow the rule, we will have a chart with words that do not follow the rule.

Soft c with e and i Hard c with a, o, and u cent Cinderella cab cob cub cinch century can cod cube cereal cinnamon car coffee cuff circle ceremony cake cold cupid circus celebrate came come cure cease certain catch cone cute cell Cindy come coal city cinch coach civic

Soft g with e and I hard g with a, o, and u general giant game goat gum gem gibber gate go Gus gest giblet gay goal gut gentle gigantic gab gone gun germ gibe gall gob gust **general gin Gary good gull George ginger gash golly gush German gist gas goof**

Note: The u in guess, guide, guitar, and guard is silent. It is there so that the g will not be next to the e or i. If it were next to the e or I, the g would have the soft sound. The y in gym is acting like a vowel

(i). guess gym guide guard guitar

G Words That Do Not Follow the Rule

The g rule states that words beginning with e and i should be soft. However, these are some of the words that do not follow that rule. It is not essential that children memorize these at this point. They just need to know that there are some words that do not follow the rule.

ge words: gi words:

geese gibbon gild gecko gift gilt get gig gird gear giggle girl geyser gill gift

A Different Approach to Reading

My experiences while teaching reading in a bilingual classroom have taught me many things. This is why I propose more credit could be given to the child's ability to learn more than one English vowel sound at a time. I believe sometimes confusion is compounded when children first learn that a vowel has a certain sound, then they go on to another vowel, and finally returned to the initial vowel only to learn that it has other sounds. Going back and forth can cause some children to believe that there is no end to it.

Instead, introduce the three sounds of "a," practice saying the sounds, and show the spelling possibilities. Students know from the onset that in reading, if one sound does not work, they are free to try another sound for that letter.

Consonant sounds can be practiced with rhyming words. One vowel family can make many words, and the only thing that is changing is the beginning consonant. This practice with rhyming words as spelling families allows students to experience success immediately. They can learn many words from cat by changing the first letter. By changing ending sounds, they make even more words. The words they are learning are actually single syllables as in Spanish. Later, they will make bigger words by combining syllables. This process will be introduced later with the spelling cvc box.

The vowel charts will get students to see and become familiar with many words, thus an opportunity to increase their vocabulary. If students are asked to write as many words as possible in a given time, they can write many more words because one simple word will bring to mind a family of words. These families are later used as their spelling words as well as in small stories.

Handy Tools Evaluating

Most of the time, the classroom teacher will let the tutor know the particular needs of a child. It is not always so obvious. The following is an evaluation the tutor can use to see if there are any concepts the kindergartner needs to develop before learning the letters and their sounds.

First, practice by using any manipulative found at home or in school such as cubes, different size cups, or different kinds of beans to sort by size, shape, color, etc. Play games and use needed vocabulary during the day to reinforce positional words (left, right, top, bottom, etc.). Use the Readiness Evaluation to assess.

If the child has a good foundation, and is ready to begin learning letters and sounds, begin with the lesson plan on page thirty-six.

Pre-evaluation

Readiness Evaluation
1. Color the objects that are the different.
2. Color the stars that are **on** the line.
3. Color the objects that are the same.
4. Color the objects that are tall.
5. Circle the objects that are small.
6. Put an x on the lines that are straight
7. Color the stars that are under the line.s
8. Circle the dots that are on top.
9. Color the arrows that point to the left.
10. Color the arrows that point to the right. Pre-Reading Evaluation

Name_____ date:_____

On-going Evaluation

The evaluation grids can be used as you are instructing, when children demonstrate that they know a letter or sound, or when they can read a list of words without prompting.

Small groups can be formed with those who are taking longer in order for the whole class to go on, but remember the whole group benefits from the practice, even if it is for the benefit of just a few. While some children are asked to read the lists, others can be asked to spell words from the list, or to write as many words s they can in a given time. They can also work with partners.

You cannot separate reading from spelling and writing. They can reinforce one another, thus sounding out while writing reinforces the way the letters are going to be sounded out in reading.

Progress Report on Consonant Sounds																				
Name	b	c	d	f	g	h	j	k	l	m	n	p	q	r	s	t	v	w	x	y	z

Progress Report on Reading Lists - A																	
Name	an	at	ad	am	ack	ag	ap	a-e	ai	ay	ei	ey	eigh	ar	aw	ar	al	wa	alk

Writing the Letters

Use these simple rules to write all the letters:

1. Begin to write the letter with the stroke on the left hand side. For example, the line in the b is to the left of the circle, so begin with the line.
2. Lines always start on the top and go down, or left to right. Slants can go left or right. They can begin at top or bottom.
3. There are backward circles and backward curves. There are frontward circles and frontward curves. Backward circles begin at 2:00. Show the children where 2:00 falls on the clock. The a, the d, the g, and the q begin with backward circles. Frontward circles are written beginning with an upward stroke on the b and the p after the line. Curves are incomplete circles.
4. Most letters end with a downward stroke on the baseline, then curve up with a puppy-dog tail right before touching the baseline.
5. Verbal cues help the child to remember. Say them out loud while you demonstrate on the board. Repeat the cues while the children practice.

Verbal Cues for Writing the Letters

a. Start at two, backward circle, up and down, and puppy-dog tail.
b. Start at topline, down to baseline, up and frontward circle.
c. Start at two, then a backward curve.
d. Start at two, backward circle, up, up, down, and a puppy-dog tail.
e. Left to right from nine to three. Up and backward curve.
f. Start at two, backward curve, down to the baseline, and cross.
g. Start at two, backward circle, down, down, and curve to the left.
h. Start at the top, down to the baseline, up, curve, down, and a puppy-dog tail.
i. Start at mid-line, down with a puppy-dog tail, and dot.
j. Start at mid-line, down past the baseline, curve to the left, and dot.
k. Start at the top, down to the baseline, stop. Start at the midline, slant to the left, then slant to the right.
l. Start at the top, down to the baseline with a puppy-dog tail.

Learning to Read in English and Spanish Made Easy

m. Start at mid-line, down, up, curve at midline, and down. Up, curve at midline, down with a puppy-dog tail.

n. Start at mid-line, down, up, curve at midline, down with a puppy-dog tail.

o. Start at two, backward circle, and close.

p. Start at mid-line, down, down, up, and frontward circle at midline.

q. Start at two, backward circle, down past the baseline, and slant up.

r. Start at mid-line, down to baseline, up, and curve to the right at midline.

s. Start at ten, backward curve, slant to the right, and curve to the left.

t. Start under the top-line, down to the baseline with a puppy-dog tail, cross at the midline.

u. Start at midline, down, curve up at baseline, up to midline, and down to the baseline with a puppy-dog tail.

v. Start at mid-line, slant down right, slant up right.

w. Start at mid-line, slant down right, slant up, slant down, slant up.

x. Start at mid-line, slant down right, stop. Start at the mid-line, slant down left.

y. Start at mid-line, down, curve up, touch the line, down, down, and curve left.

z. Start at the midline, slide to the right, slant down to the left, and slide to the right.

Writing Practice

Spelling

The cvc Box

Use the cvc spelling form on page 36 to practice spelling and to evaluate progress as you go from chart to chart.

This form can be used for as long as the children need it. The form will force them to focus on the vowel and vowel family.

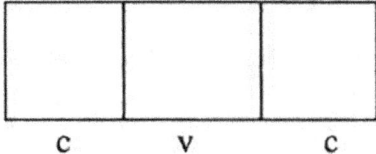

In this box, a vowel is always, always placed in the middle. The syllable can be open, where consonants are missing before and/or after the vowel. They can be closed, where two consonants surround the vowel. But the syllable must always have a vowel. If the children understand this, they are less likely to omit vowels when spelling or writing stories.

You might want to introduce the cvc box now or at any other time you feel is appropriate. You can use laminated sheets so that the students can fill in the blanks. This goes a long way to help those children that do not hear all the sounds.

The rule is that the beginning consonant or consonant blend, if there is one, goes in the first box. The vowel, or vowel family, goes in the middle box. The ending consonant letter or consonant group, if there is one, goes in the last box. The cvc box helps tremendously in spelling. It allows children to stop and concentrate on the vowel sound because there is a box there for that vowel. Later on, longer words will require more than one box—one for each syllable.

- Place the "silent e" outside the box to show that it has no sound.
- Since the ay and the aw make the sound of a, they go together in the vowel box.
- The alk is broken up because there is a consonant sound to the alk family.

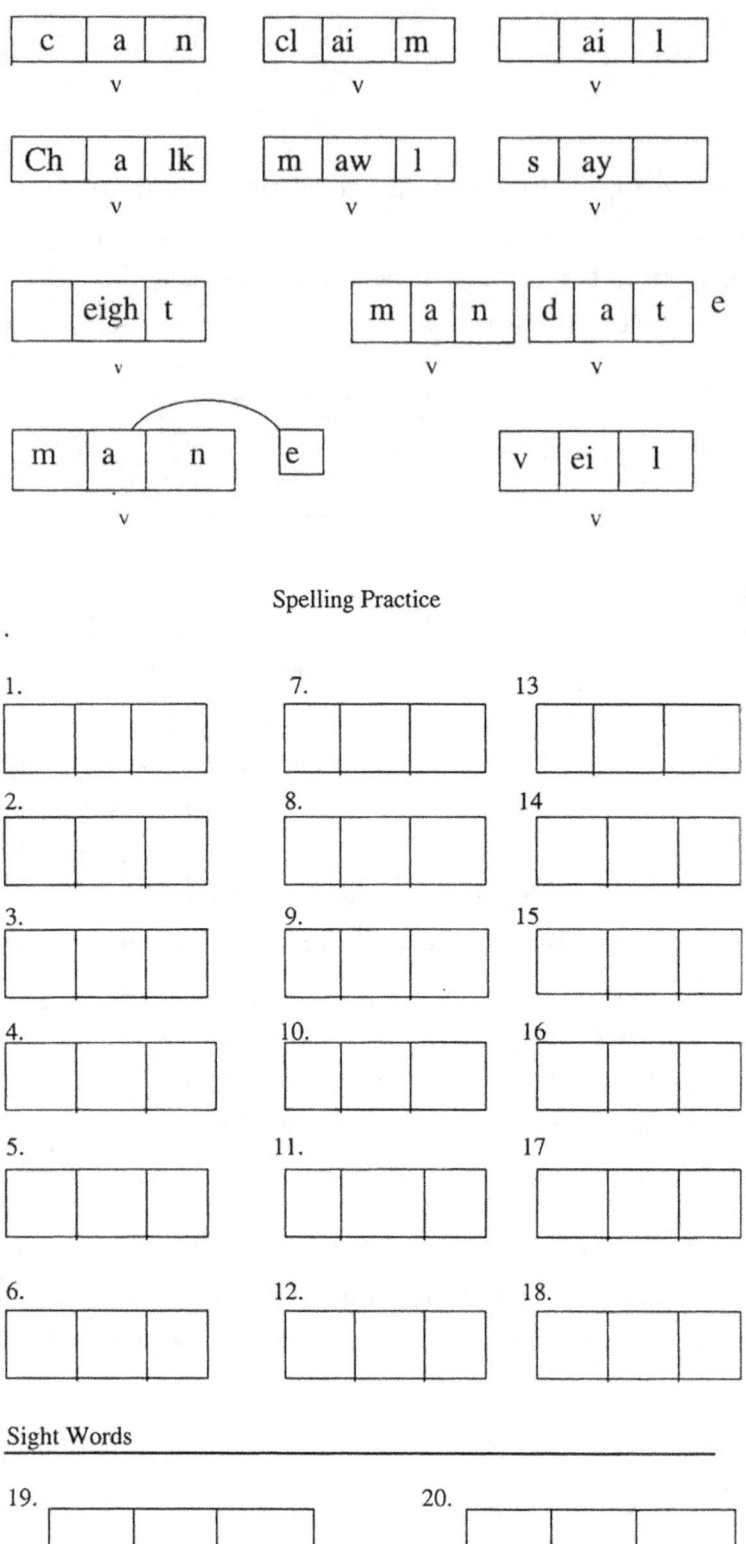

c	a	n
v

cl	ai	m
v

	ai	l
v

Ch	a	lk
v

m	aw	l
v

s	ay	
v

	eigh	t
v

m	a	n	d	a	t	e

m	a	n	e

v	ei	l

Spelling Practice

1.
2.
3.
4.
5.
6.
7.
8.
9.
10.
11.
12.
13.
14.
15.
16.
17.
18.

Sight Words

19.
20.

Possible Weekly Schedule

Monday	Tuesday	Wednesday	Thursday	Friday
Review alphabet	Review alphabet	Review alphabet	Review alphabet	Review alphabet
Introduce chart #1	Review chart #1	Review chart #1	Review chart #1. Say different ways to spell the a sounds.	Review chart #1 Say different ways to spell the a sounds
Introduce Chart #2. Point out spellings in words.	Chart #2 Review 3 sounds of a in words.	Chart #2 Review 3 sounds of a in words	Chart #2 Review 3 sounds of a in words.	Chart #2 Review 3 sounds of a in words
Chart #3 Review beginning consonant sounds in chart ... Model reading an words: ex. mmm with at makes...mat. Next, give cues, and children say the word.	Chart #4 Review beginning consonant sounds in chart. Read an words. Model reading at words:	Chart #5 Review beginning consonant sounds in chart, Read an, at, words. Model reading ad words.....	Chart #6 Review beginning consonant sounds in chart, Read an, at, ad, words Model reading am words....	Charts #3,4,5,6 Review beginning consonant sounds in chart, Read an, at, ad, am words. Model reading ack words....
Practice writing an words if ready. If not, use the writing cues for writing a, c, d, .backward circle letters, see p. 45	Practice writing at words if ready. If not, use the writing cues for writing a, c, d, g, o, q Backward circle Letters, p.45	Practice writing ad words if ready. If not, use the writing cues to write b, f, h, k, l Tall letters p.45	Practice writing am words if ready. If not, use writing cues to write a, n, t, b, d, f, J, and l	Practice writing ack words. Use writing cues to write a, n, t, b, d, f, j, l, and m.
Practice spelling by writing an words in cvc box. Until children are able to spell, model spelling on cvc box on board	Practice spelling at words in cvc box	Practice spelling an and at words in cvc box	Practice spelling ad words using cvc box.	Practice spelling am words using cvc box.

Planning for a Lesson

Depending on the children, the time allotted, and the time of the year, you may select from the objectives below.

Objectives: Children will: (Select one or more)

__ demonstrate they know the names of all the letters of the alphabet by reciting the alphabet forward and backwards while pointing.
__ know and recognize the five vowels.
__ say the three / two sounds of the vowel: _a, _e, _i, _o, _u
__ read rhyming words by changing the first letter. (col. 1) family____
__ read words with given vowel family.
__ read a short story using words in chart. _____(vowel families)
__ spell rhyming words with the _____(family)
__ spell words with given vowel family.

Vowel Family Spellings:

__a __ a-e __ai __ay __ey __ei __eigh __e __ea __e-e __ee __ea __ey __-y __i __i-e __ie __-y __o __ough __o __o-e __oe __oa __ow __ough __o __oo __ou __ough __u __u-e __ue __ew __ui

Review

(About three minutes) Depending on the time of the year, learning the alphabet may be your sole objective. Eliminate this step once all the children know all the letter names.

1. Recite the alphabet while pointing to the letters.
2. Evaluate one or two students by having them recite the alphabet backwards.
3. Recite the vowels and point out that every single word HAS to have a vowel.

Introduce with Chart #1

Use Chart #1 to introduce the "a" sounds. The three sounds of the a are repeated many times—" Øa" (apple), "a-" (apron), "ä" (autumn), " Øa", "a-", " ä"— while pointing to the chart with its different spelling possibilities. With daily repetition, the sounds are memorized. They can later quickly be used to figure unknown words.

At this point, talk about the tongue placement, the mouth formation, the use of teeth, lips, and tongue, and the difference between voiced and unvoiced sounds if necessary. A letter is voiced if a vibration is felt in the throat area while saying the sound. Some examples of voiced letter sounds are lll, mmm, nnn, rrr, and vvv. The unvoiced letters make sounds that come out of the throat smoothly with no vibration. Have children put their hands on their throats to see if they can feel the vibrations in a voiced sound.

This helps bilingual children especially. For example, the sound of the letter z is like an s, but voiced. Point out that the sound of the letter t is made with the tongue pressing harder in Spanish than in English. Some letter sounds are made with the use of the tongue or the placement of the tongue in a particular place.

Demonstrate with Chart #2

Chart #2 is used to show **where** the vowel family falls within the word, and to practice **saying** the vowel sound in the words. Repetition of the different sounds aids in retention.

Practice with Charts #3, 4.

Charts #3, 4, etc., are used to practice reading lists of rhyming words or lists that use a particular vowel spelling.

Vowel Lessons Using Charts

Introduction–Chart #1 (About five minutes)

Discuss these points before reading chart:

1. Short vowel stands alone to make the short vowel sound.
2. Two vowels together can make one vowel sound (ai).
3. Some consonants go with a vowel to make a vowel family (alk).
4. Sometimes you hear the consonant, sometimes you don't (eigh).
5. There is more than one way to spell vowel sounds in columns two and three.

- Say the sounds of the vowel as you read across.

Demonstrate–Chart #2 (About ten minutes)

- Repeat sounds. Point out how the vowels and vowel families fit into the words.
- The first column will have short vowel sounds and the second column will have long vowel sounds. The third column has the "third" sounds of the A, O, and U. (The third column is set up so that if there is a fourth sound, as in oo, words having like sounds are grouped together in different charts.)
- Repeat the sounds **and** words in the first two rows until the children can repeat the two rows rhythmically. Tell children that first, you will be using the word patterns from row one to make many words. Later, you will be using the word patterns from the other rows to make even more words.

Practice–Charts #3, 4, etc. (Can be used to practice consonants)

- Repeat the sounds at the top. Practice the beginning consonants from the rhyming words in the first column by using the associations for consonants beginning on page 19. Point out those sounds in the rhyming words. Help children locate words that do not rhyme, if any.
- Read the rhyming words from the first column with the teacher.

- Point out that the first column has the same vowel sound, the same vowel spelling, and the same ending sound. All they have to do is change the beginning sound to make rhyming words. Give them the rhyming family (at) model reading down the column. Children repeat. As children are ready, evaluate individually as they "read" the words on their own or read the words randomly as you point.
- Use the Progress Chart for Consonants to check off the known consonant sounds. When the students can say all the short-vowel words in the first column of the "A" charts, they will have encountered all the consonants as beginning sounds. If you notice, the child is not learning the beginning consonant sounds in isolation but within the context of a word. In this way, the child does not have to undo a bad habit of reading sounds in isolation.
- At this point, you may chose to stop and introduce all the short vowels using the same steps thus far before continuing.
- Read the second and third columns with long vowel sounds and third vowel sounds as children are ready.
- Read sentences using vowel families.
- Read stories using vowel families.
- Spell and/or write rhyming words.
- Spell and/or write words with vowel families.

Review—(About two minutes)

Ask : What vowel family did we learn about today? Tell me two ways to spell the long sound of a. Who can spell _____? Why are we learning vowel families? (To make words and learn to read)

Evaluate—

Children say the sounds of the vowel independently. Use evaluation charts to mark off as children show mastery.

Things to Remember About the Charts

1. It is not necessary that the children learn the words immediately. They will be reviewing the words for several days.
2. The short vowel is found with no other vowel.
3. The long "a" with the "silent e": The e is like a super hero. It has the power to go **back** over one **and only one** consonant to make the vowel call out its name. What I would do is role play this with children. They each hold a card with a letter (make long a words with silent e). The arm of the child holding the e goes over the consonant next

to it and nudges the first vowel. (Whisper: "Call out your name!") The "silent e" then puts his hand over his mouth to show that he is silent. Practice this by changing the vowel and making new words.

4. Spanish speaking children who are learning English tend to say "ah," which is the Spanish a. They are familiar with the short e sound, so get them to say eh, and open their mouth and throat wider to say Øa.
5. The long a sound is compared to the ei in Spanish.
6. The third column words make the **third** sound of a. In Spanish, the sound and mouth formation are about the same, but the throat is tighter in English and more relaxed in Spanish.
7. Repeat this chart until the children can say the sounds fluently.
8. Read down the short vowel column in order to practice the beginning sounds. Most words will be rhyming words, but as they are ready, add different endings when possible. By the time all the short vowel charts are learned, the child will have gone through all the consonants.
9. To increase vocabulary, go over the meaning of the words and use them in sentences. Whenever possible, act out some unknown words.
10. Learning beginning sounds by using rhyming words helps to practice the whole word fluently, instead of a sound at a time. As every teacher knows, this is very important when reading. You do not want the children to read letters, but whole words. Fluency helps the child to better concentrate on meaning.
11. When most of the children can call out the words, it will be time to go to the next line of "a" words. This solidifies the sound of the short a, and also makes them focus on the different ending sound. When they realize this pattern, the other charts go much faster.

Chart 1a - Ways to Spell the Three Sounds of A

Short a Long a Third sound of a a a-e aw a ai au a ay ar a ey al a ei wa a eigh alk a a a

Sight Words the is I to a on has in

Chart 2a - See the A Spellings in Words

Short a Long a Third sound of a a a_e aw

rat rate raw

a	ai	au	man	mail	maul
a	ay	ar	pad	pay	par
a	ey	al	ham	they	hall
a	ei	wa	back	vein	want
a	eigh	alk	wag	weigh	walk
a	a	a	zap	able	about

Chart 3a - Practice the A Sounds in Words - Øa, a-_e, aw

a -_e aw at ate awl bat date bawl fat fate fawn hat hate hawk cat Kate jaw lat late law mat mate maw pat plate paw rat rate raw sat sate saw vat gate yaw that dawn

Chart 4a – Practice the A Sounds in Words – Øa, a-i, au

a ai au an ant ail auk ban band bail auto can cans pail cause Dan dank jail daub fan fang fail fault pan pant hail haul ran rang rail laud tan tank tail Paul man hand mail maul San sang sail Saul Nan land nail van lank wail
Practice ending sounds only after mastery of beginning sounds.

Chart 5a – Practice the A Sounds in Words – Øa, ay, ar

a -y ar bad bay bar cad clay car dad day dark fad Fay far had hay hard lad lay lark mad may mark pad pay park sad say start Tad stay tart clad x-ray are

As children are ready, add blends (bl), or digraphs (ch, sh, th, wh). Teach the word **are** as a sight word. It has a lazy silent e, because it does not make the a call out its name.

Chart 6a – Practice the A Sounds in Words – Øa, ey, al

a ey (a-) al am all bam bey ball cam Mey call ham hey hall dam Rey fall jam they gall lamb hall Pam mall ram pall Sam stall yam wall

Note: If a word ends with the l sound, the l is usually doubled at the end of a short word. Ey is at the end of a word, ei is in the middle of a word.

Chart 7a – Practice the A Sounds in Words – Øa, ei, wa

a ei wa back lei want black beige wad crack deign wan flack feign want hack reign wash Jack rein wasp lack seine watch Mack veil water pack vein watt quack

Note: Other wa words:
1. Wax is following the short a rule.
2. Way is following the long a rule of ay
3. Wake and waver are following the silent e jumping over one consonant to make the vowel call out its name rule. Was has the wu sound. It does not follow the rules and should go to the corner to think about it. A giggle usually follows.

Chart 8a – Practice the A Sounds in Words – Øa, eigh, alk

a eigh (a-) alk bag eight walk crag neigh balk drag neighbor chalk flag freight stalk gag weigh talk hag weight walk lag sleigh Mag nag rag sag wag

Chart 9a – Practice the A Sounds in Words – Øa, a-, a (uh)

a

-

ₐ a (Y) **(uh)**

cap able about clap acorn ago dap agent agree flap alias ahead gap alien alive lap amen around map aside nap rap zap

Note: Even though most words that begin with "a" as a syllable have the (uh) sound, there are times when the letter "a" will have the long vowel sound as a beginning syllable.

There will be no sentence practice for these words.

Reading Practice with A: at , a_e , aw

- Nat ate a date.
- Nate is late.
- Draw a cat that sat in a vat.
- The bat has a jaw.
- The fawn pats the paw.

- I saw the rat on the gate.

The Rat at Dawn: Story with a, a_e, aw

At dawn, Kate sat to draw a cat. Kate saw a fat cat that sat on a mat. The fat cat saw a rat on a gate. The rat saw the fat cat. Scat rat!

If needed, ask student to repeat the three sounds of a to figure a word.

Reading Practice with A: an , ai , au

1. Saul saw the mail in a pail
2. Paul can sail at dawn.
3. The auk is at the rail.
4. The ant can haul a nail in a jail.
5. It is Jan's fault.
6. The man can haul the lamp.

The Ants: Story with a, ai, au

Paul sat on a pail. The pail had ants. The ants cause Paul to wail. Paul ran to Saul. Saul and Paul can bang the ants in the pail!

Reading Practice with A: ad , ay , ar

1. Fay had a bad day.
2. I say that the car can stay in the park.
3. Start the mark on the hard pad.
4. Dad is smart.
5. May I stay in the dark?
6. The jar is in the hay far away.
7. Are Tad and Sam mad at the lad?

The Hard Day: Story with a, ay, ar

Fay is in the dark. Mom is mad at Fay. Dad is far away. Fay is sad. Fay had a bad day!

Reading Practice with A: am , ey , al

1. Call Sam at the mall.
2. The tam on Pam can fall.
3. Jam is on the wall.
4. Hey! They ate all the ham.
5. Rey is tall.
6. Mey ate the last yam.
7. They may call to paint the wall.

The Ham: Story with a, ey, al

Mey and Rey are in a jam. They ate all the ham. They call Sam at the mall. Sam gets ham, jam, and yams at the mall.

When the l is at the end of a word, it is usually doubled.

Reading Practice with A: ack , ei , wa

1. Wash the black veil.
2. The crack was in the beige wall.
3. Mack lacks water.
4. The wasp is back.
5. I want a red lei.
6. Jack has a watch.

The Veil: Story with a, ei, wa

Jack wants to wash the beige veil. Mack wants to watch. Jack lacks water. The veil can stay black.

Reading Practice with A: ag , eigh , alk

1. Drag the eight rags.
2. Weigh the tall stalk.
3. The bag has chalk.
4. The flag has a tag.
5. I can talk to the hag.
6. The cat can walk and wag the tail.
7. The nag can neigh.

8. The weight makes it sag.

The Neighbor: Story with a, eigh, wa

Mag has a neighbor. The neighbor wants to talk. Mag wants to play a gag on the neighbor. Mag drags a bag of chalk. The neighbor wants to weigh the bag. They talk and walk and drag the bag.

More practice with A sounds.

Dan's Date: Story with A Sounds

Dan had a date. It was at the park. Dan the man was late. Was it Dan's fault? The car had a flat. Dan saw that it was past eight. Call for a haul, Dan. It was a bad day.

Can Dan take a train? Can Dan sail? Can Dan wait? Hey, Dan can walk to the park. Start to walk, Dan. Walk to the park. That is Dan's fate: to walk to the park at eight.

Chart 1e - Ways to Spell the Two Sounds of E

Short e Long e
- e e e e_e e ee
ea ea e ey e y

Chart 2e – See the E Spellings in Words

Short e Long e
e e met
e e_e Ed eke
e ee den deer
ea ea read real
e ey help key
e y men many

Chart 3e – Practice the E Sounds in Words – Øe, e-

e

-

e bet be get he met me wet she jet we let

net
pet
set
yet
best
rest

Chart 4e – Practice the E Sounds in Words – Øe, e_e

e e_e bed eke fed fete Jed here led mere
Ned mete red Pete Ted Zeke wed scene

Ed
bend

Chart 5e – Practice the E Sounds in Words – Øe, ee

e ee Ben bee den Dee fen flee hen free Jen see Ken keep lend deer men jeer
mend queen pen green ten seem

Chart 6e – Practice the E Sounds in Words – Øea, e-a

ea ea dead ear bear dear pear fear tear tear wear flea head hear
dread real lead lead read read
bread dream meant mean

Chart 7e – Practice the E Sounds in Words – Øe, e-y

e ey check key deck monkey fleck donkey heck honey neck money peck wreck

Note: Remind the students that they also found ey as long a.

Chart 8e – Practice the E Sounds in Words – Øe, y (e-)

e y bell any cell Danny dell many fell nanny
knell candy sell dandy tell handy
well Mandy yell Benny shell Jenny help penny

1. When two words are spelled the same, but have different meaning, they are called homographs (read, read).

2. When two words have the same pronunciation but different meaning, they are called homonyms (red, read).
3. The y at the end of a two-syllable word says the long sound of e.

Reading Practice with E - e-t,

1. He is wet.
2. Get the pet to me.
3. We can let the vet rest.
4. She met me.
5. He can be in the jet.

The Pet Rat: Story with et, e-

The pet rat is in the car. Fay met the pet rat. She had a net. Can we get the pet rat wet? Not yet, 'cause the fat cat came. The pet rat ran away. He ran fast to the barn. We can get the net to get the pet rat. We can set the pet in the net. Get away cat! Get away! Get away! He ran as fast as a jet. The pet rat ran back in the car. We are glad.

Reading Practice with E - ed , e_e

1. Pete can get a bed.
2. The bed is here.
3. That is a fete.
4. Zeke is a Crete.
5. Ted has a mere dent.

Jed the Cat: Story with ed, e_e

Jed the cat is here. Pete met Jed the cat. He led Jed the cat to Zeke. Zeke is in the red bed. Zeke fed Jed the cat in the red bed. Get Jed the cat! Jed the cat ran to Pete. Pete let Jed the cat get away!

Reading Practice with E - en, ee
1. I see Ben.
2. The fen is deep red.
3. The bee gets the men.
4. The seed is three feet deep.
5. The deer can get the hen.

Ben and the Hen: Story with en, ee

Ben is a man. He has a green fen. Ben the man has a red hen. The bee gets the hen. Ben can see the hen flee. The hen flees to the queen. The queen set the hen free. The hen ran to Ben the man. He can keep the hen.

Reading Practice with E - Øea, e-a

1. I can read. He read to me.
2. The flea eats a pear.
3. She can hear the bear.
4. I fear the beast.
5. I meant to tear the bread.

The Beast: Story with Øea, e-a

We hear the mean beast. We walk to the rear. I dread the beast. The beast is a black bear. We read that we can be a real meal to the bear. We get bread to the mean bear. A flea gets the bear in the ear. The bear gets weak. Dear me! Let's get away. We shed a tear. Oh no! It was a mere dream?

Reading Practice with E - eck, ey

1. The donkey is at the deck.
2. Check on the monkey.
3. The fleck is on the neck.
4. The key is real.
5. I had money.

The Red Key: Story with eck, ey

A donkey has a red key. The red key is on the donkey's neck. The monkey is on a green tree. The monkey gets on the donkey's back. He checks the fleck on the key. The fleck has honey. The monkey pecks the sweet honey on the key. The donkey is a wreck. Can we help the donkey?

Reading Practice with E - ell , y

1. She can sell a bell.
2. Many men fell.

3. Benny yells at Mandy.
4. Jenny had a shell.
5. Randy helps Danny.

Let's Help Mandy: Story with ell, y

Mandy is handy. She has candy to sell on the deck. Benny tells Mandy to get any shell to sell. Then Mandy fell on a small shell. Mandy is not well. Can Benny help Mandy? Benny gets Jenny to help. Randy is here to help Benny and Jenny. They help Mandy sell the candy on the deck.

Chart 1i—Ways to Spell the Two Sounds of I

Short I Long I i i i I i i_e i ie i igh i y

Chart 2i – See the I Spellings in Words

Short Ø Long -

i			
i	i_e	kit	bite
i	ie	big	tie
i	igh	hip	high
i	y	sing	my

Note: Since the igh makes one single vowel sound, it is considered a vowel family and so is not broken up in the cvc box. The y makes and sound of a long I at the end of a one syllable word. The s is often doubled at the end of a root word.

Practice sentences by referring to the chart.

Chart 3i – Practice the I Sounds in Words

Ø

i i_e it bite bit bike hit hide is dire his tire in wire fin fire tin tile win mile if rile with mine

Chart 4i – Practice the I Sounds in Words – Øi, ie

Ø
i
i

‾ e big die dig fie fig hie gig lie jig pie
mig vie pig dried rig fried
twig fries

Chart 5i – Practice the I Sounds in Words – Øi, igh

Ø
i
i

‾ gh dip high drip fight flip light grip might hip night lip plight nip right tip sight rip tight trip thigh

Chart 6i – Practice the I Sounds in Words – ing, y (i)

Ø

i, y (ˉ) king by sing my ping dry ring fly sting fry thing ply bring pry cling shy fling sty sling try wing why

Reading Practice with I - it, i_e
1. A fish has fins.
2. The bike is mine.
3. She bit the tail fin.
4. He hit me with his bike.
5. The fire is a mile away.

The Fire: Story with i_ , i_e ,

Tim is on a fine bike. He is with his dad. They see a big fire. The fire is far away. Tim rides his bike three miles. A tire hit a tin can. The tire got a flat. This is dire! We can not get to the fire. Get on the wire and get help fast.

Reading Practice with I - ig , ie
1. She will lie in the rig.
2. The pies are big.
3. We ate all the fries.
4. He has dried the twig.
5. I tried to eat the fig pie.

Sam the Pig: Story with ig , ie

Sam the pig is big. He bit a big pie. The pig tried to eat all the fries. He can not dance a jig. He is big and fat. He can sit in a dig. He will not fit in a rig. The pig can lie on all these twigs. He can lie here to sleep.

Reading Practice with I - i , igh

1. My grip is a bit high.
2. The cat likes to nip my thigh.
3. I might take a trip.
4. She was right.
5. Why did he lie to me last night?

What a Sight!: Story with ip and igh

Flip takes a trip at night. He gets on a green car. He takes a right at the light. Wait! The car might hit a big rock and slip. The car flips high in the air. Will Flip get a tight grip? His car falls on a tire. This is a plight. Flip hit his lip. The lip is a sight. Flip is all right.

Reading Practice with I - ing , y (i)
1. My big ring shines.
2. Take that thing away.
3. Bring me a dry bat.
4. Why cling to a bad thing?
5. Try to make the kite fly.

The Sad King: Story with ing and y

The king is shy. He wants to fly high. Bring me my wings to try. The wings are by the spring. The wings are wet. The king tries to fly with wet wings. He falls. His arm is in a sling. The king is sad. He will sing by the spring.

Chart 1o - Ways to Spell Three Sounds of O

Short o Long o Third Sound of o
o o o - oo
o o-e oo
o oe ui
o oa ou
o ow ew
ough ough ough
o old oo

Chart 2o – See the O Spellings in Words – Øo, o-, o - (oo)

Short o Long o Third sound of o
-
o(ä) o o - (oo) cot go do
o o_e oo cob cove fruit
o oe ui sock hoe cool
o oa ou cod boat you
o ow ew bond low brew
ough ough ough bought though through
og old oo dog bold look
-
o o o - oo
cot Bo do
dot fro to
got go who
hot ho boo
jot Jo coo
knot no goo
lot so moo
not too
pot Woo
rot choo
shot
trot o o-_e oo
Bob bone boot
cob cope cool
gob dome fool

glob grove goose
job joke loop
mob mole moon
rob robe root
pop poke pool
crop Rome room
hop sole goose
shop shone shoot
stop stone stool

Chart 5o – Practice the O Sounds in Words – Øo, o-e, ui

o o-e ui (oo)
Block doe fruit
Clock foe suit
Dock hoe cruise
Flock Joe bruise
frock Moe
hock roe
jock toe
lock woe
mock floe
rock
sock

Chart 6o – Practice the O Sounds in Words – Øo, o-a, ou

o o-a ou (oo)
cod boat you
clod coat could
God foal would
mod goat should
nod goal route
pod load soup
rod moan toucan
sod moat youth
Tod bloat wound
Sight word: of

Chart 7o -Practice the O Sounds in Words - Øond, o-w, ew

ond o-w ew (oo)
bond blow blew
pond crow crew
fond flow flew
grow grew
mow mew
know knew
row drew
snow new
throw threw

Chart 8o -Practice the O Sounds in Words - ough (Øo, o-, oo)

ough o-ugh ough (o-o-)
ought though through
bought dough
brought
fought
sought
wrought
thought
Sight words: rough, tough

Chart 9o – Practice the O Sound in Words – Øog, o-, oo

og o oo
bog only book
clog okay crook
dog obey hook
fog ogre look
frog oh rook
hog bolt took
jog colt foot
log dolt good
nog jolt Hood
old
bold

Reading Practice with O - Øo, o-, o-oo
1. This is not too hot.
2. Who can say, "Ho, ho, ho" and "Boo"?
3. Do not see the knot.
4. The pot will not rot.
5. Who will not go to the zoo?

The Tot that Got Hot: Story with Øot, o, o-oo

It was a hot day. The tot got so hot. Who can help him? What will we do? He will not go with me. Let's go to Dot. Dot got the tot wet in the pool. Now the tot is happy.

Reading Practice with O - o , o_e , oo
1. Bob made a joke at school.
2. Rome is too far away.
3. Do not poke me in the knee.
4. She will not go home.
5. I can not cope with the mob at the pool.

The Note: Story with o , o_e , oo

Rob got a cool note in the mail. Bob said, "Let's go to the zoo." So Rob and Bob went to the zoo. There was a dome. It was a home for bats. Bob said, "Boo" to Rob. Ooh! Let's go home and tell jokes.

Reading Practice with O - ock, oe, ui (oo)
1. The flock of geese is near the doe.
2. Do not mock me.
3. Soon, we will go on a cruise.
4. The hoe is by the rock.
5. Lock it with a key.

Late: Story with ock , oe, ui

Moe sees the clock. He is late to school. He zooms past a flock of geese. He zips past the dock. His class is in line to go in. He goes so fast, that he hits his toe on a rock. Moe takes off his sock. It is a bad bruise, so he has to go back home.

Reading Practice with O - od, oa, ou (oo)
1. The rod is next to the goat.

2. The goal of the team is to win.
3. Could you eat the hot soup?
4. Would you take the rod with you?
5. The youth will get in the boat.

Story with od , oa , ou (oo)

The billy goat got a pea pod. Rod came in a boat. He could see the billy goat run with the pea pod. Would you please stop? That pod is mine.

Reading Practice with O - ond , ow, ew (oo)
1. The crew will tow the ship.
2. Mow the grass.
3. I can chew.
4. The throw was too low.
5. I want to know who drew this.

Story with ond, ow, ew

It rained. The grass grew. It had dew. When it dries, I will mow it by the pond. Then, a crow came. I knew that he flew too low. He fell on the grass with dew. Can he eat the grass? Can he chew it? He is not fond of it.

Reading Practice with O - ough, ough, ough
1. I ought to get through.
2. I thought this was right.
3. He bought this with his money.
4. She tried, though she could not do it.
5. He brought a lot of dough to make cookies.

Making Cookies

The man bought a lot of dough to make cookies. He thought he was through. He ought to go fast. So he sought help. He brought Sam to help make cookies.

Reading Practice with O - og, old, oo
1. The dog is too old.
2. The bold frog took the gold.
3. The hog is cold.
4. I want to hold the hook in my hand.

5. Look who sold the good book.

The Dog Who Bit A Crook

There was a man who loved his dog. He told the dog to sit. The dog would not obey. They took a jog in the fog. Then, a crook took a good book from the man.

Oh, no! The dog bit the foot of the crook! Good dog.

Chart 1u - Ways to Spell the Three Sounds of U

Short U Long U Third Sound of U u u_e (yoo__) u_e(oo__) u ue (yoo__) ue (oo__) u ew (yoo__) ui (oo__) u eu (yoo__) u (oØo)

Chart 2u – See the U Spellings in Words

Short U Long U Third Sound of U u u_e (yoo__) u_e (oo__) bug cute rude
u ue (yoo__) ue (oo__) bun cue rue
u ew (yoo__) ui (oo__) but few fruit
u eu (yoo__) u (o
Øo) bus feud put

Chart 3u - Practice the U Sounds in Words - Øu, u--e, u-e (oo)

u	_e (yoo__)	u_e (oo__)
up	cute	brute
us	cure	crude
bug	duke	dune
dug	fume	fluke
hug	lure	rude
jug	mule	tube
lug	puke	tune
mug		dude

Note: The yoo and the oo sounds of u can both be written with a silent e.

Chart 4u - Practice the U Sounds in Words - Øu, u-e, ue (oo)

u	ū-	e	(yoo__)ue	(oo__)
bug		cue		blue
rug		due		clue
trunk		fuel		flue
skunk		hue		glue
bulk		slue		rue
fuzz		true		Tuesday
cruel				

Chart 5u – Practice the U Sounds in Words – Øu, ew, ui

u	ew	(yoo)	ui	(oo)
but	dew			fruit
cut	few			cruise
gut	knew			bruise
hut				mew
jut				new
mutt				pew
nut				skew
rut				spew
Yew				

Notes: view has the sound of yoo, so the I can be explained as silent.

Chart 6u - Practice the U Sounds in Words - Øu, eu, u (oo)

u	eu	(oo__)	u	(oo__)
bust	feud			bull
crust	feudal			full
dust				tull
just				pull
lust				push
must				put
rust				tulip
trust				tuna

Reading Practice with U - u, u_e (yoo__), u_e (oo__)
1. You are so cute.
2. Hey Dude! Can I get a hug?
3. The Duke is on the mule.
4. Can you cure me?
5. A bug is on the sand dune.
6. That was a fluke.
7. He dug a hole in the sand dune.
8. He needs a lure to fish.
9. The mule can lug the big jug.
10. Get a tune for us.

Reading Practice with U - u, ue (yoo__), ue (oo__)
1. The bug is blue.
2. The clue is in the trunk.
3. Is it true?
4. Can it wait til Tuesday?
5. She is due back at three.
6. I am low on fuel.
7. The blue rug is too bulky.
8. The fuzz on the duck has a blue hue.
9. I rue the day that I fell.
10. I can smell the skunk.

Reading Practice with U - u, ew (yoo__), ui (oo__)
1. Sit on the pew.
2. The cat will mew for you.
3. The hut is not new.
4. I got a bruise on my leg.
5. We went on a cruise last Tuesday.
6. I got a few nuts, but I can not eat them.
7. I knew that the fruit was good for you.
8. The yew is a tree that is always green.
9. A few drops of dew are on the grass.
10. The mutt has a gut.

Reading Practice with U-u, eu (yoo__), u (oØo)
1. I just want a tulip.
2. I do not trust the bull.

3. Do you like tuna?
4. I must pull the weeds.
5. I just want the feud to end.
6. Put the dust in the trash can.
7. We must push hard.
8. The hook is rusty.
9. Eat all the bread crust.
10. Do you trust me?

Building for the Future

If children see these words daily, they will expand their visual memory for words. The important thing at this point is to read the words fluently. You are building for the future.

It was always important to me that I not tell children an unknown word, but gave them the tools to figure it out themselves. Whether one is practicing reading word lists or reading stories, having the phonetic tools to figure out a word is 100 percent better than being given the word outright. If children practice words in families, they will use the same strategy to figure out similar words. There is no need to be told over and over again if they are able to figure out the word themselves.

The above consonant letter groups can be said to follow some kind of rule because they belong to a family. There are actually just a few situations that do not follow some kind of rule. You just have to know the rule. For example, the reason the words *serve* and *move* have a silent e at the end is because there are no words in English that end in v. Proper words from other languages can end with v (Slav), but English words do not end with v. So if a v sound is at the end of a word, an e follows it.

Here are some charts with other vowel families:

Other Vowel Families Charts

The er, ir, and er are the **/er/ girl triplets**. They have a cousin ear as in earn and wor in word.

Bert	bird	burn	Earth	word
derby	dirt	curl	earn	work
fern	first	fur	learn	world
germ	girl	hurt	pearl	worm
herd	Kirk	lurk	search	worth
jerk	mirth	murk	yearn	worry
nerve	sir	spurn		
perk		turn		
serve				
term				

The ear as in earn has a consonant after it which differentiates it from bear. The exception to this rule would be the word *heart*

Chart 7: The Spanish-speaking children will have to practice making the er sound more than the English speaking children. They will tend to sound out the vowel instead of just allowing the r to overpower it.

boy	boil
coy	coin
joy	doily
annoy	foil
ploy	hoist
royal	joist

toy   moist
noise

Chart 8: For bilingual students, the oi sound is familiar and is written the same way. If you sound out the o and the i in Spanish, it will come out with exactly the same sound as in oy in boy.

I pretend to pinch the skin in the back of my hand and say "ouch" to remind children of the ow sound. To help them figure out a word, I do the same pinching motion without saying a word.

The cOW said "OUch"

bow	about
cow	bout
down	cloud
frown	found
gown	ground
howl	hound
jowl	joust
now	loud

town sound Chart 9: The ow (long o) and the ow as in cow are practiced by going down the row, then switch to read horizontally for a challenge.

Long o¯ ow in cow

bow	bow
bowl	brow
grow	gown
glow	how
low	jowl
mow	now
know	pow
row	prow
sow	sow
tow	town
vow	

Note: The ow sound in English is similar to au in Spanish.

If the child knows that ow can have two sounds, they will figure out the right word better as they are reading. If one way does not make sense, then they can try the other.

The ou presents a similar problem, so we will practice a few of these

Ou in cow ou (oo)
ouch could
out would
our should

bounce you Note: The ou in touch does not follow the rule and the ou in journey is connected to the r which overpowers the vowel sound.

Sometimes, two vowels put together will sound out both letters:

bias create boa via dual geometry theater

Endings to Root Words

Endings can be added to root words. The usual endings of s, es, ed, ing, and er are taught in first grade. I will discuss these only, but the rules in spelling words with endings will be the same with the other endings.

As a tutor, children usually come to me not knowing why a spelling rule applies. So I try to simplify it in terms they will understand. These are some of the explanations I have used with children from first to fifth grades:

The s or the es ending is added to words to make them plural. The s and es endings are also added at the end of vowels in the third person while conjugating verbs. The ed ending signifies a past action and the ing ending an ongoing action. The er ending and the est ending are used when comparing two objects (big, bigger, biggest), or two actions (fast, faster, fastest). It also signifies a person who does a certain action (sing**er** is the person who sings).

There are some spelling rules that effect the way the words are spelled without having to go into a complete spelling lesson, the simple spelling explanations below have worked very well with students I have tutored.

rush rush *es* rushing rushed

The es follows the root word instead of an s because the final sound of words that end with s, z, sh, and ch have to be separated from the s sound because they sound too much alike.

step steps stepping stepped

The p is doubled because if it is not, the i in ing or the e in ed will reach over the one p and make the e call out its name. We don't want ste-ping with a long e, so we double the p to make the second vowel far enough from the first vowel. Remember, the silent e goes back over one and only one consonant to make it call out its name? The rule does not only apply to the silent e. Any vowel can go back over one and only one consonant to make the vowel call out its name.

run runs running ran runner

Some verbs like ran are called irregular verbs because they do not follow the format of most verbs where past tense is signified by an ed ending.

large larger largest

When an ending is placed after a word with a silent e, the silent e in the root word is dropped because it is replaced by the e in the ending. The job of the silent e in large was to make the g soft, but now the e from the ending can do that job. If it were to be left in the word, there would be two vowels next to each other (largeer) and so the first vowel would have to call out its name.

happy happier happiest

When a word ends with a y acting as a vowel, the y first changes to an i, then the er or est ending are added.

Conjugating Verbs

Many times it is helpful in a bilingual classroom to conjugate some verbs in order to help children with grammatical errors. In first grade, I would mostly discuss the differences in the placement of the s ending. Since it is different in English and Spanish, I conjugate a few in order to help them with their grammar and their writing.

English Spanish

I run. We run. Yo corro Nosotros corremo *s*
You run You run. Tu corre *s* Ustedes corren
He run *s* They run. El corre Ellos corren.
She run *s*
It run *s*

The important thing to show here is that the s ending is not only to make plurals, but it is at the end of verbs. I point out that in Spanish the s is not in the third person as in Spanish, but in the second person singular and the first person plural. When children relate what they don't know in their second language to something they do know in their native language, the transition to English is smoother.

Making Complete Sentences

I made a bulletin I considered extremely effective. In order to get children to write better sentences independently, I made sections with parts I wanted the children to include in their sentences. Some children have a hard time getting started. They just sit there with a pencil in their hands. They need a boost to get started.

We were learning about nouns as a name of a person, place, or thing and verbs as action words. So I combined everything into one. All they had to do was select words from the subject columns and from the verb column to make a complete sentence. Then to make the sentence better, they could add the when where and why words..

Select from subject and from verb to make a sentence.					Select these to make it better.		
Subject					Predicate		
Nouns				Verb			
Person	Place	Animal	Thing	Did What?	When?	Where?	Why?
I You Mom Teacher	My house The school The park San Antonio	The lion My cat Rusty A tiger	The chair My book The tree The color	ran broke tore read	today now yesterday Someday	at home next door in the box on top	because ,,,,,

How to Make a Sentence

To make meaningful sentences, students select a subject, then a verb (action word or is, was, etc. as a state of being. For higher level sentences, add the when, where, and why. Keep adding words to the table as needed.

Spanish Reading

Spanish reading is very uncomplicated. The spelling is much more consistent and the vowels have only one sound. The letter c and g can both have the soft sound (-ss, -h), when followed by the e or the i, or the hard sound (same as in English), when followed by the a, o, or u.

In Spanish, you teach the vowels first.

Vowels

a (ah) like English ahh
e (eh) can be stressed
i (ee) like in meek
o (oh) stop short of making it a long o
u (oo) like in tool
y (ee) when used as a vowel

Consonant Sounds that Are Different from English

There are no consonant digraphs in Spanish of (th, sh, and wh).

The letter c and the letter g each have two sounds, as in English. The soft sounds of the letters c and of g are made when they are followed by an e or an i, and the hard sounds of c are made with the a, o, and u.

ca ce ci co cu (kah) (se) (si) (ko) (koo) The hard sound of the letter g can also be made when it is followed by an e or an i sound however, and this is where it differs from English. The g has to have a silent u next to it in order to make the g hard with the e or the i.

Hard g's (The sound is like the hard g in English)

ga gue gui go gu

Soft g's (The sound is like an h sound in English).

ge gi

The q is only written with a silent u and the e and the i.

que (ke) and qui (kee).

The letter h is silent.

The letter j sounds like an English h.

The ll (eye) sounds like the y in yes.

The ñ is like the n sound in onion.

The r is strongly trilled at the beginning of a word, or when preceded by l, n, or s. In all other positions, the tongue taps once lightly.

The rr (erre) is a strongly trilled r.

The k is found only in words of foreign origin.

The x can sound like the English x, like the Spanish j, or like the s.

The z is like the English s.

Charts for Spanish Reading

The syllables in Spanish words follow the same cvc rules as the English words. Syllables can be open or closed syllables. The vowel dipthongs are not broken up unless two strong vowels separate to make two different syllables or if an accent on a weak vowel separates it from a strong vowel. More about that later.

Lu nes mar tes miér co les jue ves sá ba do

U no dos tres cua tro cin co

Sie te o cho nue ve diez dí a

Using a chart with syllables of all the consonants, children can begin to make words simply by putting the syllables together. As in English, most texts begin with the m, s, and t syllables to make words then sentences. Reading Practice with Syllables – m , s , t

a e i o u
ma me mi mo mu
sa se si so su
ta te ti to tu
am em im om um
as es is os us

Sentences with m, s, and t syllables
Mi mama me ama. Este osito es mio.
Soso se asoma. Esta es mi mesa.
Susi se mete. Tu me asustas. Reading Practice with Syllables - n, p, l

na ne ni no nu
pa pe pi po pu
la le li lo lu
an en in on un
al el il ol ul

Sentences with n, p, l, m, s, t.
Mi Mami toma té. Tu mono está en la loma.
Su pelo es liso. Papi puso la mano en la mesa.
El último es Memo. Papá me pasa la masa.
Estamos en el piso. Salta en la sala.
Antonio tuvo la tos. Manuel es alto. Reading Practice with Syllables - d, r, f

da de di do du
ra re ri ro ru
fa fe fi fo fu
ad ed id od ud
ar er ir or ur

Sentences with r, f, and **d**
La rana se fue para afuera. Dáme la peseta.
¿Tienes un sarape? Màndalo a la tienda.
Le da miedo a la rana. Nené no se duerme.
El lodo está duro. Rosalinda es famosa.
El se sale de la sala. Mamita se ríe fuerte.
Nos fuimas a la fuente. La forma es redonda. Reading Practice with Syllables – b, h, ll

ba be bi bo bu
ha he hi ho hu
lla lle lli llo llu
ab eb ib ob ub

Sentences with b, h, and ll words.
Los osos no son feos.
La huerta está absolutamente bella.
El animal amarillo se fue a la llanura.
Mamá le da besos a su bebito.
La ardilla no esta dormida.
La bellena está en el mar.
Las pasas están en la tina. Reading Practice with Syllables – rr, ch, v

rra rre rri rro rru
cha che chi cho chu
va ve vi vo vu

Sentences with rr, ch, v
La rana corre con la chiva.
La muchacha se va arriba de la chimenea.
Me tomo todo mi champurrado.
El es muy chistoso. Me hace reír.
Vámos con mi abuela a la tienda.
Vanesa baila la cumbia con su hermano. Reading Practice with Syllables – g and j

ga gue gui go gu
ge gi
ja je ji jo ju

Sentences with g and j
Me gusta el guiso.
La guitarra se me perdió en el jardín.
Mi familia nada en el golfo.
El general es mi guía en la guerra.
El gato gordo no se puede dormir.
Guillermo es mi buen amigo. Juego mucho con él.
A José le da gusto estár en el jardín.
Julia toma jugo de naranja. Reading Practice with Syllables – c, qu, y

(C is soft like an s when followed by an e or an i)

ca que qui co cu
ce ci
ya ye yi yo yu

Sentences with c, q, and y
¿Quién puso mi yoyo en la yarda?
Celia se quita guantes amarillos.
Alberto se queda con su cucharra.
Mamá quiere su chequerra cuando va a la tienda.
Yolanda es mi hermanita chiquita.
Mi mamá y mi hermana se llaman Lucy.
Quita la yuca de aquí. Reading Practice with Syllables – k, z, x

ka ke ki ko ku
za ze zi zo zu
xa xe xi xo xu

Sentences with k, z, and x
Se venden periodicós en el kiosco que está en la plaza.
El camino a la playa es cincuenta kilómetros.
Mi abuelo tocó el xilófono en la boda de mi tía.
Mis zapatos rojos me quedan chicos.
Conozco a Mónica muy bien. Vowel Dipthongs in Spanish
Vowel diphthongs are made by combining vowel sounds. The final y when a part of a diphthong is treated as a vowel.

ai, ay (like a long I sound) aire, hay
au (like ou in out) auto
ei, ey like long a sound) reina, ley
eu (ay oo) Europeo
oi, oy (like English oy) oigo, soy
ia, ya (like ya in yard) distancia, yarda
ua (like wa) cuando
ie,ye (ye like yes) yema
ue (like oo e) fue
io (like yo, yo
uo (like in quote) cuota

iu (like yu) ciudad
ui (like wee) cuidado

The i and the u are considered weak vowels. The strong vowels (a,e,o) are the ones that are stressed normally. If this rule does not apply in the word, then the weak vowel is accented (í,ú) to show that it is to be stressed as a separate syllable (Maria). In iu and ui, u and i are both weak, so they are stressed equally. Likewise, two strong vowels are stressed equally (ua).

Spelling with Syllables

Words are made up of syllables just like in English. The syllables can be opened (ma) with a vowel having only one consonant on one side, but not on the other. It can also be opened by having no consonants at all. The syllable can be closed (com) with a vowel having a consonant or consonant blend on either side.

v v v
v v v
v v v

Accent Rules for Spanish Words

1. Words that end in a vowel, n, or s, stress the next to the last syllable.

2. Words that end in a consonant (except for n or s) stress the last syllable.

    These are the two rules for words when they are stressed naturally, with no accent. If a word does not follow these rules, and stresses a different syllable, then you have to put an accent in order to show which syllable to stress.

3. All words stress only one syllable, except for adverbs ending in mente. In words ending with mente (ly in English), the stress of the original is retained, and the stress of mente is added.

4. Aún has an accent when it takes the place of todavía.

5. Words that ask a question or that exclaim (¿Cuándo?, ¿Quién?) (¿Cómo?) have an accent to show stress.

6. The vowels i and u are accented when they are preceded or followed by another vowel and form a separate stressed syllable (María, baúl).

7. The conjunction o takes an accent when it comes between two Arabic numerals to avoid mistaking it for a zero (3 ó 4).

8. An accent is used to distinguish between two words that are spelled the same, but have different meanings.

   él (pronoun) el (article)
   tú (pronoun) tu (possessive adjective)
   mí (pronoun) mi (possessive adjective)
   éste (pronoun) este (adjective)
   ése (pronoun) ese (adjective)
   aquél (pronoun) aquel (adjective)
   sí (pronoun or adverb) si (conjunction) sé (verb of ser and saber) se (reflexive pronoun)
   más (adverb) mas (conjunction)
   dé (from the verb dar) de (preposition)
   té (noun) te (pronoun)
   sólo (adverb) solo (adjective)

9. Words ending with a vowel, n, or s stress next to last syllable *nat- urally,* so they do not need an accent because they are following rule naturally.

   Words ending with a consonant not n or s stress the last syllable *naturally,* so they do not need an accent because they are following the rule naturally.

   Words that need an accent are those that do not stress the vowel naturally. They do not follow the rule, so you have to show which vowel to stress.

   ll**e**vo divid**i**r drag**ó**n **a**bro **a**bril div**á**n **c**ome abord**a**r d**ó**lar **sa**len com**e**r f**á**cil **co**rres bond**a**d s**á**bado d**u**da flu**i**dez **á**rbol

   j**ue**gan leal**ta**d com**í**

   Use these exercises as needed and in the order that is most beneficial to you and your student. Everyone coming to a tutor has to be taken as an individual with individual needs. Hopefully, this book will be used to fill in some gaps for those children who depend on us to help them catch up with their peers.

   Whether we are teachers, parents, tutors, volunteers, friends, or individuals wishing to practice our reading skills, I am sure that these practice charts and ideas can help.

In today's world, one cannot get away from reading. It is essential in every aspect of our lives. Having a strong foundation in reading will enable individuals to teach themselves. Good readers enjoy reading for pleasure. It can also develop the imaginations of young readers. Strong readers increase their vocabulary. Good readers are free to concentrate on detailed reading for better understanding. Good luck, and keep reading.

www.ingramcontent.com/pod-product-compliance
Lightning Source LLC
Chambersburg PA
CBHW081406070526
44583CB00020B/2694